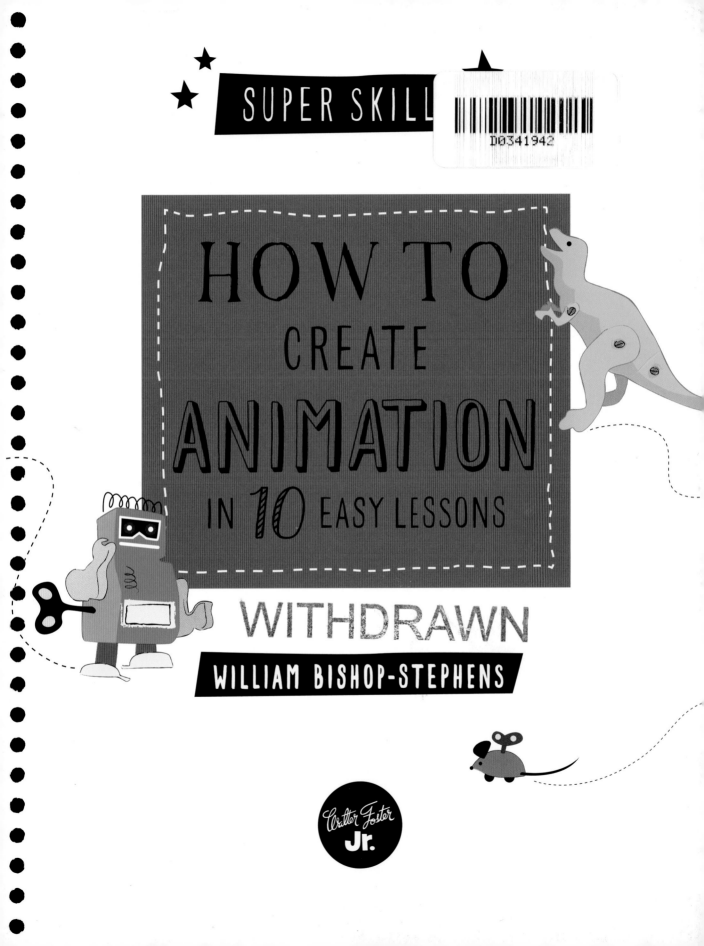

SUPER SKILLS

D0341942

HOW TO CREATE ANIMATION
IN 10 EASY LESSONS

WILLIAM BISHOP-STEPHENS

Walter Foster Jr.

ABOUT THE AUTHOR

Will Bishop-Stephens is a freelance animation director and writer as well as a lecturer at the University of East London and previously the Royal College of Art. He's worked on a number of animation projects and had work shown at international film festivals. Will has 14 years' experience leading animation workshops for children and young people.

Quarto is the authority on a wide range of topics.

Quarto educates, entertains and enriches the lives of our readers—enthusiasts and lovers of hands-on living.

www.quartoknows.com

Part of The Quarto Group
The Old Brewery
6 Blundell Street
London N7 9BH

First published in the UK in 2016 by QED Publishing

Published in the USA by Walter Foster Jr.,
an imprint of Quarto Publishing Group USA Inc.
All rights reserved. Walter Foster Jr. is trademarked.

Publisher: Maxime Boucknooghe
Art Director: Susi Martin
Editorial Director: Laura Knowles
Design: Kevin Knight
Original Illustrations: Joanna Kerr

6 Orchard Road, Suite 100
Lake Forest, CA 92630
quartoknows.com
Visit our blogs at quartoknows.com

Printed in China
1 3 5 7 9 10 8 6 4 2

CONTENTS

INTRODUCTION

SO YOU WANT TO BE AN ANIMATOR?

Animation is amazing! It can be used to bring movement to beautiful, detailed drawings or make two blobs of modeling clay fight. You can create a disaster movie starring your favorite toys, or even make your best friend disappear. Anything you can imagine, you can animate! In this book, you will discover the 10 skills needed to become an expert animator. Before you know it, you'll be making everything from fairy tales to sci-fi epics!

WHAT IS ANIMATION?

"Animation" is the trick of bringing something to life with the illusion of movement. The illusion is created when a series of still images, which differ slightly, are flashed before the viewer's eyes. The brain sees the series as one moving image.

WHAT YOU NEED:

To turn an animation into a moving image on a screen, you'll need a smartphone, tablet, or computer or laptop. You'll also need some animation software.

WHICH SOFTWARE SHOULD I CHOOSE?

There is a lot of free and affordable animation software available. Type "stop-motion" into your app store to access a free or low-cost animation app. It's essential that the app has a function called "onion skinning," which allows you to arrange still images into a series, and a feature to play back your animation.

ALWAYS ASK PERMISSION FROM AN ADULT BEFORE YOU BUY OR DOWNLOAD ANYTHING FROM THE INTERNET.

SOFTWARE BASICS

FRAME RATE

When you open your software, it may ask you what frame rate you want to use. Each still image is called a "frame," and the "frame rate" is the speed the software will play back the images.

The frame rate is measured in frames per second, or "fps."

For example, to make one second of an animation at 12 fps, you would need to create 12 frames. Most stop motion animation is captured at 12 fps.

ONION SKINNING

When you're capturing a frame, you will see a live view of what's in front of the camera and a "ghost" image of the previous frame. This is to help you line your frame up with the previous one. This feature is often called "onion skinning," after the transparent skins of an onion.

TIMELINE

The "timeline" is a series of images that makes up the animation. It usually allows you to delete or duplicate an individual frame.

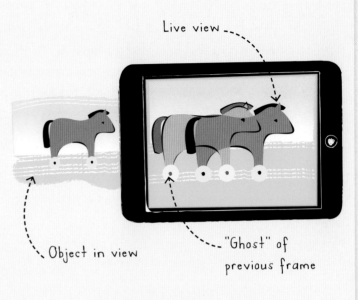

Live view

Object in view

"Ghost" of previous frame

In many apps, you can tap the camera icon to go back to animating.

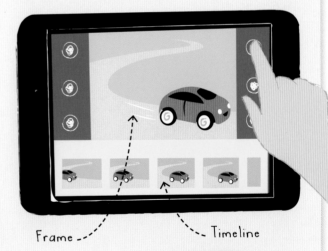

Frame

Timeline

DON'T PANIC!

If all this sounds too complicated, don't worry! You will find out more about editing software on page 56. You can also find definitions of technical and unfamiliar terms in the Glossary on page 63. By the end of the book, you'll be able to amaze your friends and family with your very own animated movies.

HANDY TIP!
Most apps have helpful videos and online tutorials that show you how to use their features.

MAKE A FLIP BOOK LOOP

The first animation most beginners make is a flip book. On the edge of a notebook, they may draw a teacher becoming a flying superhero, then flick the pages to animate the action. In this section, you will learn how to create a flip book, photograph it, and animate it. You will then loop it so it plays forever. It's the simplest form of digital animation!

- -

GETTING STARTED

All you need is a set of pages that can be flicked with your thumb. On each page, draw an image. When you flip the pages, each image is replaced by the next almost as soon as you see it, creating the illusion of movement.

If you have a small notebook or a pack of sticky notes, you can skip ahead to page 8. If you only have a sheet of printer paper, find out how to make a flip book on the opposite page.

"WOW" FACTOR!

SOME OF THE FIRST MOVIES EVER MADE WERE SEQUENCES OF IMAGES MOUNTED ON A BIG WHEEL. THE OPERATOR TURNED A HANDLE TO FLIP EACH IMAGE AND WATCHED AS IT WENT PAST A VIEWING HOLE. ONE SUCH MACHINE TO APPEAR IN AMERICA WAS THE "NICKELODEON" (NICKEL THEATRE). PEOPLE PAID A NICKEL TO TURN THE HANDLE AND WATCH THE MOVING PICTURES.

WHAT YOU NEED:

- Plain printer paper
- Small binder clip or stapler
- Large scissors
- Colored pens
- A creative brain

HOW TO MAKE A 16-FRAME FLIP BOOK

To make a flip book from a sheet of paper:

1. Grab a sheet of plain printer paper.

2. Fold it neatly in half, lengthwise.

3. Fold it again, lengthwise

4. Fold it in half, at the middle.

5. Fold it yet again. (Yes, that's four folds!)

6. Attach a binder clip or stapler to one of the shorter sides to fasten the folded paper together.

7. Use large scissors to cut through the folds on the remaining three sides. You might need an adult to help with this.

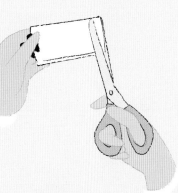

Fold four times.

Clip or staple the short edge.

Cut off the folds on the remaining three sides.

HANDY TIP!

One of the best ways to flick is to hold the clipped edge of the flip book in your hand. Press the other side of the book against your thumb so the book is bending, and flip the pages away from your thumb, a page at a time.

DON'T WORRY IF IT'S JERKY!

You should be able to flick through the pages smoothly from back to front. You might need to flatten the edges of the pages so they don't catch and jump frames. If it is still a bit jerky when you flip through it, don't worry. When you photograph the frames of your animation, you can hold each page open in turn. The app will create the movement. Now turn the page to learn how to draw and capture frames.

DRAWING AND PHOTOGRAPHING FRAMES

Once you have your blank flip book, you are ready to start drawing the frames of your animation. You will draw a different stage of the action on each page to form the frames. So what do you draw to make a great animation? This is where your creative brain comes into play!

IDEAS FOR YOUR FIRST ANIMATION

- A stick person walking up stairs
- A bee landing on a flower
- A flying saucer vaporizing a planet
- A windmill turning
- An anvil falling on a person's head
- A person biting an apple

HANDY TIP!
Go wild! The wackiest ideas are often the best. If something doesn't work, think of it as practice and try again.

ANIMATORS HAVE A SAYING: "THE MAGIC HAPPENS BETWEEN THE FRAMES." THIS IS BECAUSE OUR BRAINS FILL IN THE ACTION BETWEEN EACH STILL IMAGE TO MAKE A FLOW OF MOVEMENT THAT ISN'T ACTUALLY THERE.

Tip 1: START AT THE BACK

Draw your first frame on the last page using a dark-colored pen or pencil. Trace your next drawing on the previous page, making a tiny change in the movement, and then a third drawing on the page before that with another small change. Keep going until you complete the action.

Tip 2: SMOOTH CHANGES

Make sure each drawing is similar enough to the previous one to trick your brain into seeing a smooth flow of movement when playing back the animation.

Tip 3: KEEP IT SIMPLE

Small, complicated movements can be confusing and difficult to visualize, so make your drawings bold and the action clear and simple.

Tip 4: CHECK YOUR SPEED

Test your animation every few frames by flipping the pages. You'll soon learn how slight the changes must be in order to make the movement smooth and believable. If the movement is too fast, the action will need to be broken down into smaller parts to make more frames. If the movement is too slow, the action needs to be completed in fewer frames.

HANDY TIP!
Many cameras have settings that allow you to set up grids in the viewfinder, which help you position the pages of your flip book in the same place.

PHOTOGRAPHING YOUR FRAMES

Now it's time to photograph each page of the flip book using your animation software. Photograph the pages in sequence so that the last page (the beginning of your animation) becomes frame 1, the next page becomes frame 2, the next 3, and so on. To keep the book open, either break it apart and lay each page flat, or hold it open with your fingers.

Keep your fingers in the same place in each frame so only the drawings appear to move. You don't need to hold the camera completely still between images—you can use the software's onion skinning function to line them up.

Photograph the pages of your flip book on a plain, uncluttered surface. That way, when the animation is played, the background will remain still instead of interfering with the action.

PLAYING THE MOVIE

It feels magical when you use animation software to make your flip book move by itself. When you play back the animation, the drawings are literally moving next to your hand! Don't worry if you don't get it right the first time, just look at what went wrong, correct the error, and record the action again. You need to be willing to make lots of versions and learn from your mistakes. Practice really does make perfect!

Tip 1: TRY DIFFERENT FRAME RATES

Try changing the speed of your animation by altering the frame rate. Remember, 12 fps is a good number for achieving smooth movement. If you drop below 8 fps, you'll start to see the separate images instead of flowing movement, and the illusion will not work.

Making large changes between frames is the most common mistake new animators make, ending up with a jumping effect. If the action is playing back too fast, make smaller changes each frame to slow it down. You will need more frames to complete the action.

Tip 2: SETTING THE RESOLUTION

Resolution is a way of describing the size of your movie. It is usually measured in pixels, which refers to the number of tiny squares of color that makes up your image. If it's possible, set your animation to a High Definition size, such as 1920 x 1080, sometimes written as "HD 1080p." A movie will appear blocky if you scale it up from a low to a high resolution, but it is fine to play a high-resolution movie at a smaller size.

HANDY TIP!

For each new project, you'll need to set up a new file in your software. If you don't, all your animations will stack up in the same movie.

LOOP IT!

Did you know you can make your animation run forever by creating a loop? A "loop" means ending your animation with the same frame you started with. During play back, the animation will jump from the last frame back to the first to keep playing.

Most apps automatically loop animation when you hit the "Play" button. You can also copy and paste frames to make them repeat as many times as you like. In some apps the "reverse selected frames" function can be used to make the action run backward. This is a great tool for creating an action such as a character bowing: you can bend them forward frame by frame, and then copy and reverse the frames to make them stand up again.

TRY THIS!

◦ Make a flip book with a looping action. Start with a circle on frame 1 and end with a circle on frame 16.

◦ Make slight changes to your circle; over 10 frames, transform it into a strange creature, lovely flower, or alien spaceship.

◦ In the last six frames, change it back into a circle.

◦ The circle in the final frame should be identical to the circle in frame 1, to complete the loop.

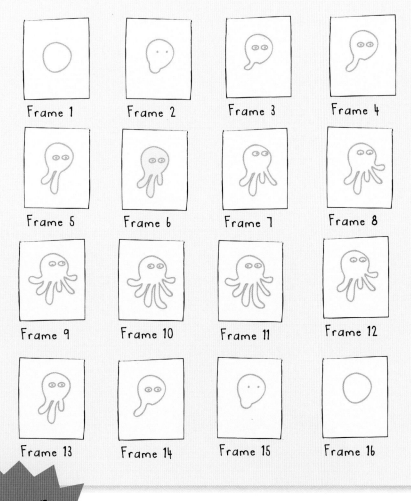

Frame 1 Frame 2 Frame 3 Frame 4
Frame 5 Frame 6 Frame 7 Frame 8
Frame 9 Frame 10 Frame 11 Frame 12
Frame 13 Frame 14 Frame 15 Frame 16

YOU WILL BE AT YOUR MOST CREATIVE WHEN YOU'RE HAVING FUN. SMILE, RELAX, AND START PLAYING WITH YOUR IDEAS!

CONGRATULATIONS!

You have now learned the basics of creating an animation. Everything else builds on this, so let's move onto the next Super Skill.

PIXILATION

A great way to make quick stop-motion animation is to use other people (or even yourself if no one else is around) as props and characters. You can make a friend ride on an invisible skateboard, drive an invisible car, or even hover above the ground. It is really fun!

RIDING AN INVISIBLE SKATEBOARD

Are you ready to make an animation of a friend on an invisible skateboard? The technique you will use is called "pixilation." It involves capturing a frame of a live actor before moving them to a slightly different position and taking a new frame. Continue this process until you complete the action.

GETTING STARTED

Find a clear area to shoot in. If you don't have a friend to film, prop up the camera so its viewfinder captures the entire area you will be moving in. Set the camera software to "time lapse" or "timer," so it takes a frame at regular intervals, then move into position for frame 1.

PIXILATION IS NAMED AFTER THE MAGICAL LITTLE PIXIES OF FOLKLORE BECAUSE THE EFFECT LOOKS LIKE MAGIC! IT HAS NOTHING TO DO WITH PIXELS.

CAPTURING THE FRAMES

◦ Stand as if you are on a skateboard and capture frame 1.

◦ Keeping your arms and legs in the same position, scoot forward a few inches. Take frame 2.

◦ Next move twice as far as you did in frame 2 and take frame 3. This will give the effect of speeding up. (You will find out more about speeding up and slowing down on pages 14–15.)

◦ Keep adding frames, moving more each time. If you're filming a friend, you can have them move around the room and around obstacles. If your camera is fixed, they will have to stay in view of it.

◦ You could end your movie by going through a doorway. An even more dramatic end might be going through a wall! Capture yourself or a friend approaching the wall a frame at a time. Once there, move the actor out of the shot and take several frames of the empty space.

◦ Every 12 pictures will give you one second of animation (remember "12 fps"). So if you want to whiz around the room for a couple of seconds, you will need 24 frames. For four seconds, you will need 48 frames.

TRY THIS!

When you've got the hang of filming your friend skateboarding, try shooting them ice skating or performing any other crazy move you can think up. Pixilation can even be used to combine live action and animated models into one movie!

HANDY TIP!
Some apps tend to play movies at 5 fps, so the action looks jerky and slow. Remember to change the setting to 12 fps. You may need to do this regularly.

SMOOTHNESS AND FLOW

So you have amazed friends with your mastery of pixilation! But how can you slow down and speed up the action while keeping nice flows of movement? In this section, we will look at the methods you can use to create smooth movement.

Tip 1: SLOW ACTION

Smaller changes per frame equals slower action. If you want to film your friend skating slowly, you'll need them to move tiny amounts per frame, so the onion skinned image of the previous frame almost completely overlaps the new image.

Tip 2: FAST ACTION

Larger changes between frames equals faster action. The size of the change depends on the type of action. For example, you can capture a jump or a punch in three frames: frame 1 shows the person getting ready to perform the action, frame 2 catches the action in full flow, and frame 3 shows the end point of the action.

Most fast action needs to last longer than three frames. When animating invisible skateboarding, for example, the skateboarder's body in each frame should be just in front of the onion skinned image. The nose of the character in the onion skinned image should be touching the back of the live-image head. If the change between frames is too big, your brain will stop linking the images up and the animation will appear jerky.

Slow   Fast   Slow

THINGS TO TRY

FLYING!

Ask your friend to jump in the air while you capture a frame. Repeat this several times, jumping on the spot, then play back the animation. If done correctly, you will see your friend hovering. You need to be patient—it's hard to capture the millisecond when both their feet are completely off the floor.

Tip 3: SMOOTH MOVEMENT

Maintaining steady changes and a consistent line of motion translates to smooth movement. The diagrams below show that smooth action depends on keeping smooth changes between each frame and staying true to the line of movement. Making small and big changes at random or going off the natural line of movement results in jerky animation.

Tip 4: ADJUSTING FRAMES PER SECOND

While it's true that a lot of animators work at 12 fps, for creating really smooth movement, you could go as high as 24 fps and make really small changes between each frame. This will slow down the action, of course.

For speeding up the action, you could play the animation at 5 fps. But keep in mind that at this speed the animation will stop looking as realistic and appear to be more like a fast slide show.

INVISIBLE CAR!

Ask your friend to sit in a chair in a driving position, holding an invisible steering wheel and placing their feet on invisible pedals. Move the chair toward the camera frame by frame, but make sure your friend stays in the same position. Start with small forward movements and steadily increase them to accelerate your car. Have your friend "crash" into the camera for a dramatic finale.

GET THINGS MOVING

Now that you've learned how to capture an action frame by frame, you're ready to animate all sorts of things. You can move objects as if by magic or bring toys to life. Anything that will hold a pose can be animated. This sort of animation is known as "stop-motion."

TRY THIS!

To get a grasp on stop-motion, set a small group of objects on a tabletop, and follow these steps to gradually bring them to life:

1 Capture a few frames of the still objects. This will set the scene.

2 Now move one object by a small amount and capture the frame.

3 Move the object a small amount again, and capture the next frame.

4 Continue making small moves with your object, taking individual frames that build up the motion, just like you did with the pixilation task.

5 Slow down movements by breaking them down into several frames, but complete fast movements in one or two frames to give them more punch.

6 Once you feel confident, start moving a second object at the same time, then add a third, and so on. Soon you'll have a host of dancing objects!

WHAT YOU NEED:

- Ordinary objects or toys
- Camera, or equivalent on a laptop, smartphone, or tablet
- Clear tabletop or desk

FIRST ATTEMPTS

While you're learning, don't worry about creating a story or a set. Just have fun experimenting with making objects come to life. As your skills improve, you will be able to add personality to toys and everyday objects.

Keep the first movies you make short and simple. That way you will spot your mistakes before you've spent too much time setting things up and capturing a lot of frames. Over time, you'll get a better feel for timing and spacing, and your animations will improve.

YOU WILL LEARN AS MUCH BY GETTING THINGS WRONG AS GETTING THINGS RIGHT!

WHOA, STEADY DOES IT!

Make sure your camera does not move when you press the button to capture a frame. If you don't have a stand, use a blob of modeling clay to hold the camera in place or tape it to a mug or box with masking tape. Look through the viewfinder to make sure the prop isn't obscuring the camera lens.

HANDY TIP!

Make a habit of capturing video or photos of anything that might be useful for animation. Write your ideas down in a notebook or the equivalent on your phone so that you don't forget them.

ANIMATING TOYS

Do you have an action figure with limbs that move into different positions? If so, you have a ready-made character to star in your stop-motion shoot. But now you also have more complicated actions to think about.

A FAST COMEDY WADDLE

A toy figure with jointed arms and legs makes a great animation puppet! Start by animating your toy waddling along until you feel confident enough to lift its legs in a more elegant walk. To make the figure waddle, move one of its legs forward as if it's taking a stride, and capture the frame. Then bring the second leg forward to meet the first, and capture another frame. Repeat this several times, and you will see a fast comedy waddle when you play back the animation.

"WOW" FACTOR!

A LITTLE BIT OF STICKY PUTTY UNDER THE FOOT OF A CHARACTER MAKES IT HARDER TO ACCIDENTLY KNOCK THEM OVER, AND IT ALSO MEANS YOU CAN MAKE THEM WALK UP VERTICAL SURFACES!

HANDY TIP!

Search garage sales or thrift stores for toys to use in your movies. You'll find lots of cheap and unusual things!

ARMS AND LEGS

Have you ever paid close attention to how a person walks? Notice how their arms move to balance the movement of their legs. The strip below shows nine stages of movement you can copy, frame by frame, to animate your toy figure. Repeat the sequence from steps 1 to 9 to produce a smooth walk.

STEP 1
Start with the figure standing still, with its arms by its sides.

STEP 2
Lift the right leg and left arm forward. Move the right arm back slightly. The figure is still standing upright.

STEP 3
Make the figure lean over slightly, so the right foot moves forward and down. The left foot starts to lift, and the left leg bends backward.

STEP 4
Place the right foot on the floor, with the left foot lifting almost off the floor. The left leg is now bent back, and the figure is almost standing upright again.

STEP 5
Move the figure forward to an upright position, with both arms by its sides.

STEP 6
Lift the left leg and right arm forward. Move the left arm back slightly. The figure is still upright.

STEP 7
Make the figure lean forward slightly, so the left foot moves forward and down slightly. The right foot starts to lift and the leg bends backward.

STEP 8
Place the left foot on the floor, with the right foot lifting almost off the floor. The right leg is now bent back, and the figure is again almost upright.

STEP 9
Move the figure forward to an upright position, with both arms by its side.

HANDY TIP!
Don't forget to use the onion skinning feature of your animation software!

STORYBOARDS AND SHOTS

Once you're confident you can move your models the way you want and capture the frames, you can start planning longer shots and stories. A "shot" is all the animation captured within a single setting while keeping the camera on the same spot. You can create a story by putting different shots together.

WHAT MAKES A STORY?

Often there are three parts to a story:

○ **The beginning** This is where we meet a character for the first time and find out about them: "Once there was a knight who stomped around shouting orders."

○ **The conflict** This is where the character is faced with a problem: "The knight was out riding when he met a giant troll blocking his path. He shouted at the troll, but the troll ignored him. It just sniffled and kept looking at one of its own feet."

○ **The resolution** This is where the character acts to resolve the problem: "The knight noticed the troll had a big thorn piercing the bottom of its foot. The knight pulled the thorn out. The troll smiled and let the knight pass."

Tip 1: CREATE A STORYBOARD

A "storyboard" is a great visual device to plan your story on paper. It is like a cartoon strip showing all the shots you'd like to film. It enables you to plan long action sequences, prepare all the things you need, and spot any problems before you begin.

A storyboard isn't meant to show every single frame of your story. It might show one panel for each shot, or a few panels if it's a shot with a lot of action. A storyboard provides an overview of the events that take place in your story, from start to finish.

YOUR STORYBOARD SHOULD TELL YOU:

○ Who the characters are

○ What they are doing

○ Where they end up

○ How they get there

Title ....
Director/s ....
Page number ......   Date ....

Tip 2: PLAN AMAZING SHOTS

Here are some shots you can use to make your animations look exciting and professional:

EXTREME CLOSE-UP

This is the most zoomed-in shot, usually on a character, and creates a dramatic effect. You can use it to show a character's emotions because their face fills the entire frame.

CLOSE-UP

In this shot, you can see some of the character's gestures, such as a shrug of their shoulders, but not much of their surroundings.

MID SHOT

This shot shows a character's upper body and their surroundings, and it can fit two characters with ease. This is a "normal" shot used in most films during scenes when characters are engaged in conversation.

OVER-THE-SHOULDER SHOT

This is a good way to show a conversation from a character's point of view. The audience only sees the back of the character's head and one shoulder; the shot makes viewers feel as if they are seeing the world through a character's eyes.

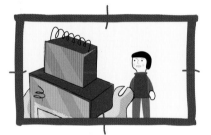

LONG SHOT

A long shot shows the whole character, the way they are standing, and any action that's happening around them.

EXTREME LONG SHOT

Here the camera is much farther away. The viewer can see the landscape the character is in. The shot establishes where a character is, what is around them, and whether they are alone or with people.

CLAYMATION

In this chapter, you're going to get a grip on one of the most fun and effective types of animation for any budding animator—claymation.

Modeling clay: the animator's enemy!

"Modeling clay is terrible stuff. It droops and falls over and changes shape. All the colors get mixed up and bits of hair and dirt always get stuck in it."

Modeling clay: the animator's friend!

"It's great stuff that bends and squashes and stays where you put it. It comes in all different colors and never dries out. You can sculpt beautiful models out of it that...oh no! It's stuck to the table!"

Both these opinions of modeling clay are valid. But keep in mind that some of the best animated movies have been made with the material, so it must be worth the trouble. The tips in this chapter will teach you skills to make the most out of modeling clay.

MAKE SURE YOU HAVE THE RIGHT STUFF!

The first step to successful claymation is making sure you are using the right type of clay.

HANDY TIP!

When you make your first few claymation characters, keep them bold and simple. If you spend lots of time making detailed characters, you might find they fall apart when you make your movie. As you gain experience, experiment with more detailed models.

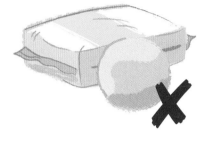

Air-dry clay and **ceramic clay** will dry out and become crumbly. Don't try to use them for animation.

Oven-baked polymer clays aren't as easy to mold and bend, even before they are baked.

Craft dough isn't the same as modeling clay—it's more springy and doesn't hold its shape as well.

Modeling clay is the ideal material for claymation. You can buy it in big one-pound blocks in art stores. It's not as squishy as the flat packs you can find in toy stores, so it holds its shape better. It's also a better value for the money.

For clean colors, get the **single-color packs**. Blue and black will stain your fingers, so it's a good idea to have some wet wipes handy to stop your fingers from dirtying the other colors.

**THE MOST IMPORTANT THING TO DO WHEN MAKING A FILM IS TO ENJOY YOURSELF! NOW.
LET'S BEGIN...**

WHAT'S IT GOING TO LOOK LIKE?

It can be tempting to spend lots of time using modeling clay to create wonderfully detailed characters for your animation. However, it's better to start practicing your claymation skills with a small ball of modeling clay, rather than spend a whole day making a fancy model that breaks apart the moment you try to move it. Here are two easy exercises to get you started.

To create your set, all you need is a large sheet of white printer paper. Prop the sheet up in a curved shape using a box, books, or a pile of magazines, as shown below.

Position your camera so that the lens has a clear view of your paper set.

Roll your blob of modeling clay into a smooth, round ball and place it in the center of the paper.

WHAT YOU NEED:

- Blob of modeling clay big enough to roll into the size of a softball
- Large sheet of white printer paper
- Clear tape
- Books or a box to prop up the sheet of paper
- Camera, or equivalent on a laptop, smartphone, or tablet

HANDY TIP!

Make sure your set is positioned at a good height in relation to your camera. The camera angle should be high enough that you can see the paper floor but none of the edges, and you shouldn't be looking directly down on the ball of modeling clay.

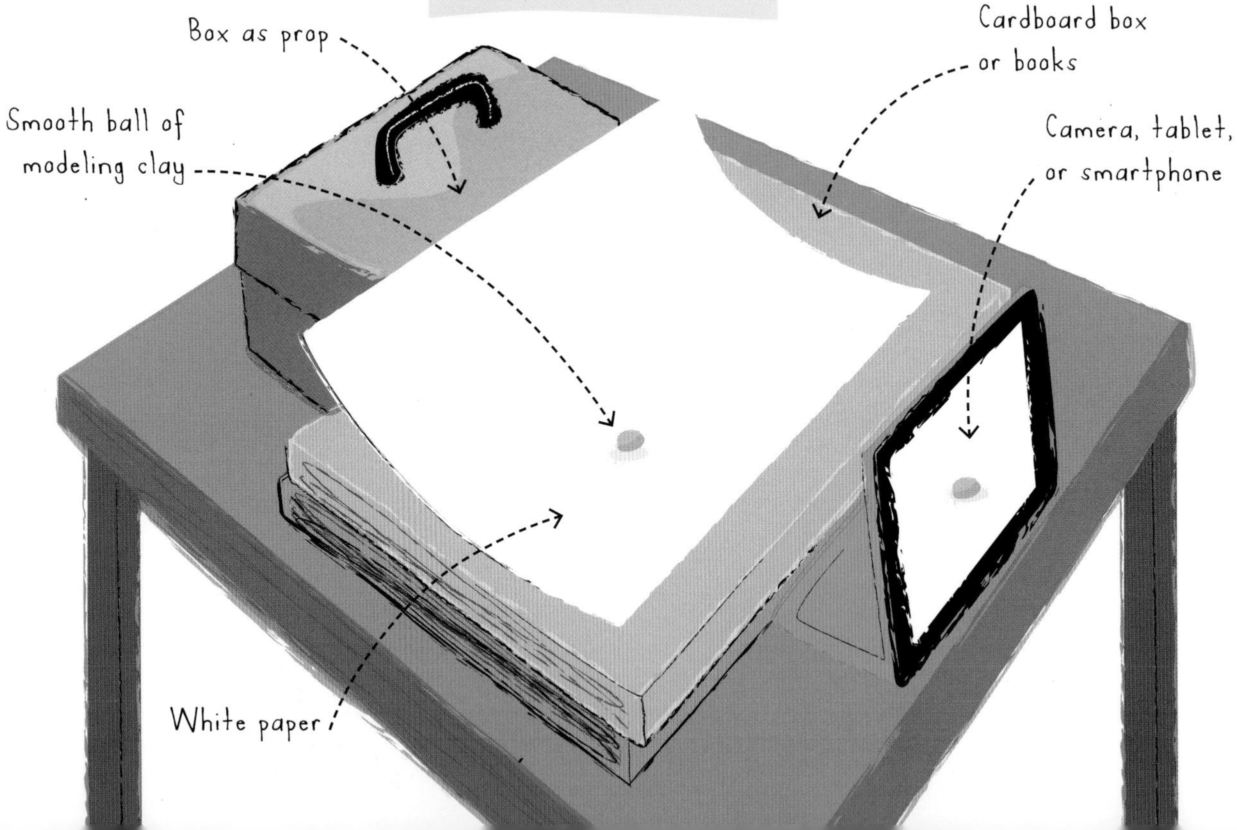

Box as prop

Smooth ball of modeling clay

Cardboard box or books

Camera, tablet, or smartphone

White paper

Exercise 1: THE "SQUASH AND STRETCH"

Now you're ready to bring your blob of modeling clay to life! The image in the camera's viewfinder should look something like frame 1.

Capture a series of six photos, molding your ball of modeling clay into different shapes each time, as shown here.

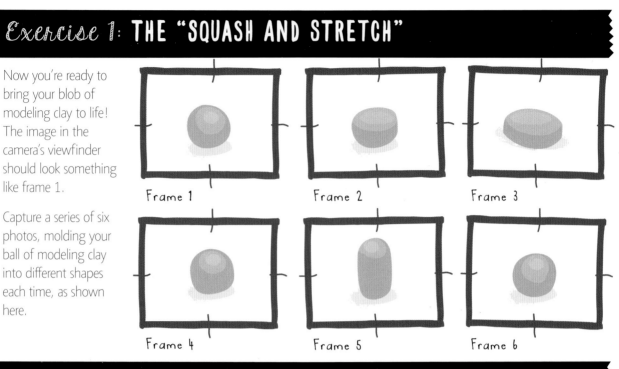

Frame 1   Frame 2   Frame 3

Frame 4   Frame 5   Frame 6

Exercise 2: THE "LEAP"

Once you have the hang of the "squash and stretch" technique, try animating your blob of modeling clay "leaping." Capture six more photos of your blob, this time molded into the shapes shown here.

Now when you play back the series of photos quickly, you will see that the blob appears to be moving! This is the basis for all claymation. The more ambitious your model and the movement you wish to create, the more time and effort it will take to animate.

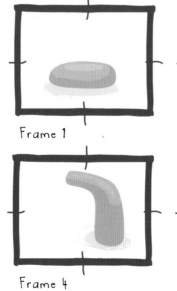

Frame 1   Frame 2   Frame 3

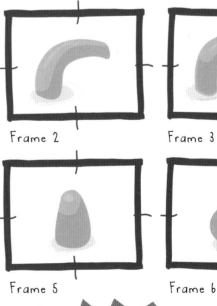

Frame 4   Frame 5   Frame 6

"ANTICIPATION" IS A CORE ANIMATION SKILL: SQUISHING AND STRETCHING MAKES IT LOOK LIKE THE BLOB IS "GETTING READY" FOR ITS BIG LEAP.

MAKING A CLAYMATION CHARACTER

The ability to make a claymation character whose arms and head don't fall off when you move them is a very important skill for animation. It's easy to do once you know how.

WHAT YOU NEED:

- Three or more colors of modeling clay (not white)
- Small white acrylic beads (alternatively, you can use white clay instead of beads)
- Clay modeling tool

BODY

First mold the shape of a hollow body by wrapping a blob of modeling clay around your thumb. Flare out the end slightly to make a bell shape that fits over the legs.

LEGS

Roll some modeling clay to make a long sausage shape about the thickness of your thumb, and bend it at the middle to form legs. Fit the body over the legs.

HANDY TIP!

Make the body and legs quite chunky. A puppet that's too tall can be wobbly. For a character who is going to move around a lot, it's best to make them short and stocky.

NECK

Roll a little bit of clay to make the neck. Then use the thin end of a modeling tool to carve a hole in the top of the body, and push the neck into the hole.

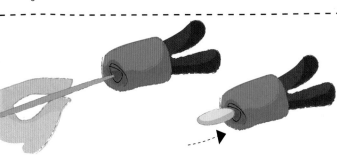

HEAD AND FACE

Roll some clay into a flat disk for the head, and push two beads into the disk for eyes. Add tiny strips of clay to make the eyebrows and a different-colored blob for the nose. Use your modeling tool to carve a mouth-shaped hole, and make another hole for the neck. Connect the head to the neck.

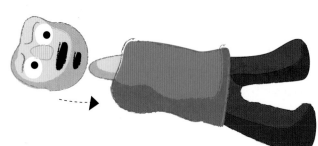

"WOW" FACTOR!

YOU CAN CREATE DIFFERENT SHADES OF MODELING CLAY BY BLENDING COLORS TOGETHER, AS YOU CAN WITH PAINT. YOU COULD MAKE YOUR CHARACTER'S EARS AND NOSE SLIGHTLY REDDER IN TONE FOR A MORE REALISTIC EFFECT. YOU CAN EVEN MAKE THESE FEATURES BRIGHT RED TO ACHIEVE A FUNNIER LOOK.

AS YOU BECOME MORE SKILLED, YOU CAN CHANGE THE SHAPE OF THE MOUTH AS YOU ANIMATE YOUR CHARACTER.

ARMS, THE WRONG WAY!

Most people attach the arms by hanging them on the side of the body... only for the arms to fall off when they lift them up!

ARMS, THE RIGHT WAY!

To fit an arm so it stays on when moved, smear the end of the arm onto the body, pressing the character's shoulder down all the way around, as shown here.

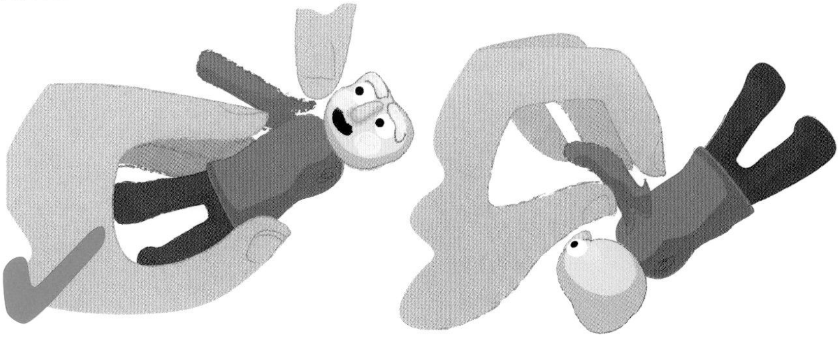

THE FINISHED CHARACTER

Ta-daa! Your moveable figure is complete! He is now ready to star in your animation. You should be able to move his arms, legs, and neck without him falling apart. Don't be too rough, though!

WHEN SHOULD YOU USE WIRE?

With a big character, you might need to use chenille stems to strengthen the limbs. The fur on the wire helps keep it from poking through the modeling clay.

If you struggle to keep your character upright, build your puppet around a length of chenille stem that goes from the top of the head and down one leg to a loop of wire in the foot. You can pin the loop down with a push pin.

THINK BIG, BUILD SMALL

Now that you know how to animate a range of objects and characters, it's time to think about your backgrounds. In this section we'll look at where to work and how you can create backgrounds for your set—in short, how to fake scale and make your characters, objects, and setting appear life-size!

WHERE TO SET UP

Here are some tips relevant to all sorts of stop-motion animation:

° A good place to set up your camera is where there aren't people or pets hanging out, so they won't accidentally knock your models over or cast shadows.

° Pushing a table or desk against a wall will give you a great starting point for propping up backgrounds and scenery.

° Choose a place where you can light your scene with artificial light rather than daylight. Slight changes in the weather will appear as flickering light in your animation. A flexible desk lamp is perfect for lighting your scene.

It's frustrating to spend time on an animation only to have it ruined. Make sure you find a safe space to work on your project.

HANDY TIP! It's possible to find a quiet corner and set up on the floor, but it's more comfortable to work on a raised surface.

MAKE YOUR OWN STUDIO

If you are really into animation, a big, stiff cardboard box is perfect for creating a versatile mini studio. A box that's about 30 inches long on all sides, large enough for standard gift wrapping paper to fit inside is ideal. Boxes made from corrugated cardboard are best, because they stay stiff. You will need to cut the top and one side of the box open, as shown below—ask an adult to help with this.

WHAT YOU NEED:

- Large cardboard box about 30 inches long on all sides
- Large scissors
- One roll each of plain white, blue, and green standard-width (30 in.) gift wrapping paper
- Sheets of multicolored printer paper
- Masking tape
- Mounting putty

Cut off the top of the box and one side

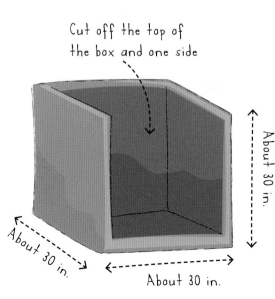

About 30 in.

About 30 in.

About 30 in.

ONCE YOU'VE MADE YOUR BOX, YOU CAN USE IT FOR ALL SORTS OF ANIMATION AND CREATE CHANGEABLE SETS, AS YOU WILL SEE IN THE FOLLOWING PAGES.

BUILDING YOUR SETS

Now that you've made your box studio, you're ready to learn the key techniques for making a miniature set. Although you are building on a small scale, you will find that you can cheat the camera to make your characters and props look huge. So it's time to think big!

INFINITY CURVE!

To create a white space that appears to go on forever, use masking tape to hang a long strip of white gift wrapping paper over the back of your box and across the floor. Don't shove the paper into the back corners. You want to gently curve it so the camera doesn't pick up the point where the floor becomes the wall (just like the simple claymation set shown on page 24). When you animate on the floor of the mini studio, it will look like your character is in an endless, featureless landscape—this is called an "infinity curve."

"WOW" FACTOR!

AN INFINITY CURVE LOOKS ESPECIALLY GOOD WHEN LIT WITH A STRONG WHITE LIGHT.

HANDY TIP!
Experiment with different colored wrapping paper to switch up your landscapes. How about blue for a river or sea, or a sandy color for a desert?

SKY AND HILLS

You can add a sky and hills and still maintain the same sense of an infinite landscape. Hang a strip of sky-blue wrapping paper over the back wall, about halfway down the spot where your curve should be. Next lay a strip of grass-green wrapping paper on the floor, about half way up the curve and overlapping with the sky. Cut the back edge of the green paper into a wavy line, and you will have created a huge grassland area and distant hills. Check out how it looks through the camera's viewfinder.

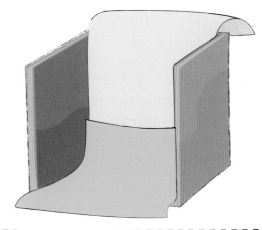

TREES AND BUILDINGS

Now you can add other features to this landscape, such as trees or buildings. Attach a flap of card stock to the back of each prop to keep it upright, and use a tiny pinch of mounting putty to keep it steady on the floor. As you build, continue to check the scene through the camera's viewfinder.

Once you start adding features like trees and buildings, you can experiment with scale and distance.

TRY DIFFERENT SIZES

Make three sets of trees that differ in size but are identical in shape—small, medium, and large.

○ Place the smallest trees at the back of the scene, placing the next size up slightly closer.

○ Keep looking into your viewfinder to see how your camera captures the scene.

○ Build the scene from back to front until your biggest trees have been placed at the front, closest to the camera.

○ Do you see how the arrangement of trees adds depth, or perspective, to your scene? You can use this trick to make your sets appear as big as you like! There are no limits!

IT'S EASIEST TO DRAW AND CUT OUT SIMPLE TREE SHAPES WHILE EXPERIMENTING WITH SIZES. YOU CAN SPEND TIME ON THEIR DETAILS ONCE YOU KNOW WHAT SIZE YOU NEED.

SMALL FAR AWAY, BIG CLOSE UP

On the previous page you discovered that you can cheat the camera so that your small set looks like a huge landscape. Now that you have a sense of how perspective works, you might find it useful to divide the set into three spaces for action: the foreground, mid-ground, and background. These three spaces aren't something you need to understand to make great animations, but they can be used to great effect if you have different-sized versions of the same characters and objects for each of the three spaces.

Foreground

In the foreground, which is the space closest to the camera, your characters fill a big part of the image. The models you create for this area have to be detailed. Try determining how much detail your camera will pick up before making your model.

You can make your foreground set with folded layers of card stock and white glue, painting on three-dimensional features. When you become more advanced and adventurous, try foam core board to make your models—foam is a great material both to paint on and carve texture into, and it will give your animation a polished look.

Mid-ground

In the mid-ground, there is less need for detail and texture. Always check the camera's viewfinder before spending hours making something that might be out of focus or hidden by an object in the foreground. If you have action that leaves the foreground before transitioning into the mid-ground, you will need to make smaller versions of your characters. That way they can leave the foreground of the shot and a smaller version of them can re-enter the mid-ground, appearing farther away.

Background

Filming action that takes place deep in the scene can look really convincing. Remember that the objects in the background are small enough that they can be made totally flat. Any characters here will be tiny too.

HANDY TIP!
Mixing painted card stock buildings with modeling clay people and toy cars can look great—anything goes in stop-motion animation!

Background

Mid-ground

Foreground

SPECIAL EFFECTS

You have probably seen plenty of TV shows and movies that have amazing special effects. These may have featured scenes in which characters were suddenly surrounded by flames, swept away by a huge wave, or performing an impossible feat such as walking on water or flying into outer space.

EXPLOSIONS

In this section, you will find out about the power of replacement animation. "Replacement animation" means swapping one object with a similar object between frames, the same way you swapped one drawing with another drawing to make a flip book, to create the illusion of movement. However, unlike the flip book, the change is sudden, and this works fabulously for creating special effects such as fires and explosions.

WHAT YOU NEED:

- Toy vehicle
- Colored paper in fiery colors such as red, orange and yellow, and green
- Scissors
- Sticky tack

EXPLODING A TOY VEHICLE

FRAME 1

Make a small, flat explosion shape out of red paper. At the right moment, such as when an oil tanker has driven into a tree, attach the small red shape to the source of your explosion. Then capture the frame.

FRAME 2

Make two larger paper explosion shapes—one in orange and one in yellow. Line up their edges and attach the shapes together to make a two-color explosion.

Now remove the red explosion shape from frame 1 and replace it with the two-color explosion, lining it up using your software's onion skinning feature.
Capture frame 2.

HANDY TIP!
Don't have an explosion at the start of a shot. You'll need about 12 frames to set the scene.

FRAME 3

Now make three really big explosion shapes: the biggest in yellow, the second biggest in orange, and the smallest in red. Make them large enough so that when placed together, they hide the vehicle that is exploding. Replace the two-color explosion with this three-color explosion, and capture the frame.

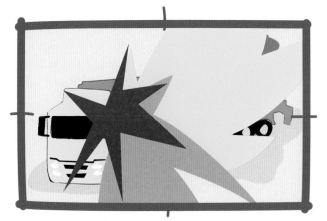

FRAME 4

Now you need to create the aftermath of the explosion, which means you will need to show the vehicle blown to pieces, with bits scattered and surrounding the center of the explosion.

HANDY TIP!
Capture several frames of the aftermath so it doesn't end before people get the full impact.

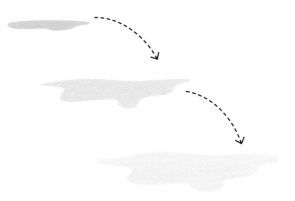

ANIMATING FIRE...

To create a fire effect, make red-, yellow-, and orange-colored flame shapes like the ones below. Fire sways from side to side, staying roughly the same size.

...AND WATER

Water becomes a puddle when the flow stops. Cut different sizes of the same shape out of blue paper, as shown below. You might need to prop up each piece so the water looks realistic. Grow a puddle frame by frame by replacing each puddle with a larger version after capturing it.

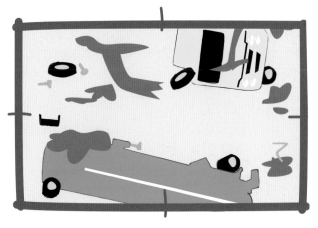

WALK, JUMP, FLY!

Making a wobbly character walk or even stand is a real problem with model animation. If your model has bendy legs and a big, heavy head, you'll need to hang it from something so it looks as if it is standing. This method also allows you to make your character jump and fly. Wowee!

A SUPERHERO FLYING RIG

Animators use a device called a "flying rig" to make characters jump and fly. The flying rig is a pole with two threads dangling from it, on which you hang your model or puppet. For a quick jump that's a couple of frames long, the pole can be supported on a frame, chair, or shelf. However, for capturing longer movements such as superhero-style flying, you want a proper rig that fits on your box studio.

HANDY TIP!
You can shade white cotton thread with colored pens so that it matches your set's background.

WHAT YOU NEED:

- Pole long enough to span the length of your box studio. You could use a tent pole, curtain rod, broom handle, or a cardboard tube.
- White cotton thread or thin fishing line
- Two squares of cardboard with a notch cut out
- Two sheets of paper to make pole sleeves
- Large scissors
- Masking tape
- Mounting putty
- Soft toy or puppet
- Pins or wire to attach threads to the puppet
- Big sheet of sky-blue paper

The two threads attach to your puppet at the head and waist to create a flying effect.

MAKING THE RIG

1. Wrap two sheets of paper around your pole to make paper sleeves, and tape them to keep them from unraveling.

2. The paper sleeves need to fit snuggly on the pole, but also rotate freely so you can wind the thread up or down.

3. Attach a thread to each of the paper sleeves with tape, so the threads hang down.

4. Use a pin or wire to attach the model to each thread.

5. Tape a cardboard pole holder to each side of the box. They will keep the pole in place.

6. If your model is heavy, use extra tape or mounting putty to keep the sleeves from unwinding.

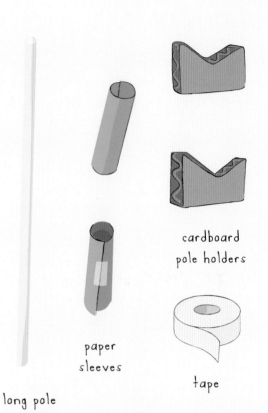

cardboard pole holders

paper sleeves

tape

long pole

HANDY TIP!

The distance between the threads should be wide enough so that your puppet doesn't spin and become tangled. The threads must also be long enough for you to lower your puppet down to the ground.

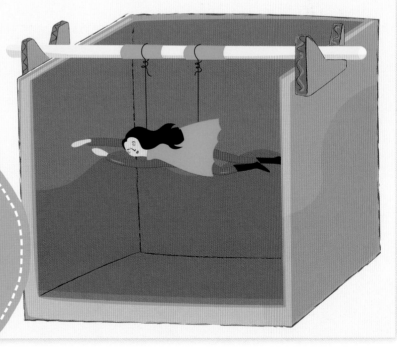

ATTACHING YOUR PUPPET

How you attach your puppet to the threads depends on whether you want it to stand and jump or fly. If you want it to stand or jump, you should push the pins into the puppet's shoulders. If you want it to fly, you will need to push one pin into the top of its head and the other into the puppet's bottom.

STANDING AND HOVERING

Now you can raise and lower the two threads by rotating the paper sleeves and fixing them at the height you want with mounting putty or masking tape. The pins must be attached at a high point on the puppet or it will flip forward.

Push the pins into the puppet's shoulders while it's lying down, and with the threads attached to the flying rig (see previous pages), you will be able to wind up the thread until the puppet is standing upright. Wind a little more, and your character will look like it is jumping or hovering.

Think back to how you made the blob jump (on page 25), crouching down and stretching up as you jump. Jump around to get a feel for what your own body looks like when you jump.

ADVANCED JUMPING!

When you jump up high, you first crouch down a little to power up for the jump. Then you push down on the ground, straighten your legs, and jump into the air.

So in your animation, start by having your character crouch down, over three frames. Unwind the thread so you have enough slack to bend the character's legs. Then straighten the character's legs, and wind the character up off the ground to nearly the top of the jump— remember, it's a sharp explosion of movement! Capture the frame. Then raise the character slightly, and capture another frame. At the top of the jump, the movement slows down. Bring your character halfway down for the next frame. Lower their feet back onto the ground for the second-to-last frame, with a slight bend in the legs. Finally, stand them up for the last frame. Play back the animation, and see how successfully you've made your character jump!

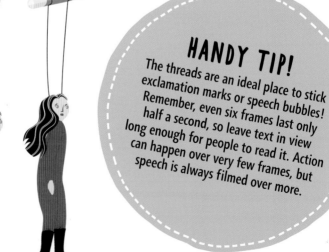

HANDY TIP!
The threads are an ideal place to stick exclamation marks or speech bubbles! Remember, even six frames last only half a second, so leave text in view long enough for people to read it. Action can happen over very few frames, but speech is always filmed over more.

FLYING FREE

To film a puppet moving through the air, put a sky-blue backdrop behind it. Use mounting putty to stick clouds and buildings to the backdrop—you don't need many clouds, because you can reuse them when they go off screen. Move the clouds backward frame by frame, so it looks like the puppet is moving forward. You can use the two sleeves on your flying rig to wind the front and back of your puppet to different heights, changing its angle to add extra movement.

HANDY TIP!
Move clouds and buildings at a steady rate. Moving a cloud by about half of its length per frame of animation is usually enough to capture smooth motion.

Place cloud in view in the background.

Lower the front thread to show the character swooping down.

Move the cloud to the left over several frames.

Move a building into view over several frames.

FILM IT LIKE A PRO

Hopefully you've had lots of fun making models, building sets, and creating fantastic animations. The techniques you are practicing are the same as those used by Aardman Animations to create their cinematic masterpiece *Wallace & Gromit* and by Henry Selick for *The Nightmare Before Christmas* and *Coraline*. In this chapter, you'll learn how animators make their movies look professional, real, and exciting.

Tip 1: DRAMATIC LIGHTING

If you want lighting that adds atmosphere to your animation, light your set with a flexible desk lamp and turn off all other lights in the room. From one side at a low angle, point the desk lamp at your set. This will create strong shadows for everything in the scene, creating a moody feel.

Lights can get hot very quickly, so be careful where you set your lamp. If possible, use an LED lamp as it stays much cooler. Keep the lamp cord away from the area you'll be moving around in to avoid accidentally bumping the light and shifting the shadows.

HANDY TIP!
You can animate the light source too! Move your light as you would a character, frame by frame. This makes the shadows move. If you are moving a character at the same time, it introduces an exciting, mind-boggling effect.

Tip 2: LOSE THE SHADOWS

To avoid multiple shadows, make sure there aren't any other lights shining onto the set. To soften the shadows, bounce the light from your desk lamp off a white surface (such as a piece of card stock) onto the set. This spreads the light and gives the scene a softer look. On professional sets, animators often mount sheets of scrap polystyrene on special stands to bounce the right level of light onto the set at the correct angle! You can also use a wall, low ceiling, or the underside of a shelf.

"WOW" FACTOR!

IF YOU BOUNCE THE LIGHT OFF SOME COLORED PAPER, YOU WILL GET COLORED LIGHT BOUNCING BACK ONTO YOUR SET. YOU CAN EVEN INTRODUCE SOME CRAZY EFFECTS BY BOUNCING A SECOND LIGHT OFF YET ANOTHER COLOR, OR HOW ABOUT SHINING LOTS OF LIGHTS, CREATING MULTIPLE SHADOWS IN DIFFERENT SHADES? TRY IT, AND SEE WHAT HAPPENS!

Tip 3: AVOIDING FLICKER

A flickering image is the enemy of any camera-based animation. Most often this is caused by failing to control the lighting, such as ignoring the subtle changes in daylight during a shoot or from people opening doors, moving around, and casting shadows on the set. Make sure not to let your shadow fall across the set, and don't wear a white top that reflects light back onto the set.

USING YOUR CAMERA

We've introduced you to some of the basics of setting up your camera. Here are some more advanced tricks of the trade that will help you improve your camerawork. You will need lots of practice and patience in order to master them, but the effort will be worthwhile.

Tip 1: CAMERA MOVES

The "camera move" is a technique where you move the camera frame by frame rather than animating a character or an object. This allows you to follow a character or reveal a part of the set that had previously been out of view. Animated camera moves are tricky because a tiny move of the camera makes a huge difference on screen. But if you can pull it off, the effect will blow your mind!

The same rules of all animated movement apply—keep the moves evenly spaced between frames and stay true to a line of movement. You will need a big set to pull off a camera move, so that you can rotate the camera around characters and objects without capturing anything beyond the edge of your set.

HANDY TIP!
Consider buying a mini-tripod to mount your smartphone or camera, rather than relying on a blob of modeling clay. There are several types to choose from—I like the bendy ones best!

HANDY TIP!
Don't let the edge of the set appear on your screen, either in a camera move or from a careless set up. It will break the magic of your animation. Nothing ruins the believability of your piece more than spotting someone doing the dishes beyond the edge of the sky!

Tip 2: FOLLOWING THE PUPPET

With this method, you follow a vehicle or character with the camera, keeping them in the center of the image and using onion skinning to line up each live image with the previous frame. While moving the camera, your eyes remain focused on the vehicle or character, so the action is less confusing for the audience.

You might try this approach when making a skateboarding pixilation. With a toy, you have more control over the movement. Move the toy first, then gently move the camera a tiny amount. Use the ghost image on your software's onion skinning feature to see when the camera lines up with the live image. Everything else will appear to have moved slightly backward, while the toy remains in the same place. Making tiny changes each time, sustain the camera move for at least five frames so that your animation captures a smooth sliding or rotating motion rather than a sudden jolt.

"WOW" FACTOR!

TRY RECREATING THE "PAUSED ACTION" EFFECT DEVELOPED BY ARTIST TIM MACMILLAN AND FAMOUSLY USED IN THE FILM *THE MATRIX*. PAUSE AT THE MOST DRAMATIC POINT OF AN ACTION—A PUPPET IN THE MIDDLE OF A JUMP, FOR EXAMPLE. THEN MOVE THE CAMERA AROUND IT IN A CIRCLE, KEEPING THE PUPPET IN THE SAME PLACE ON SCREEN USING THE ONION SKINNING FEATURE.

FANTASTIC WORLDS

Every animated movie has its own look, its own logic, and follows its own set of rules. You can think of this as the world of your movie. This means that as long as you stay faithful to the world, you're free to build fantastical sets full of detail, or make a rough set with objects you have found around the house.

WHAT'S YOUR WORLD LIKE?

If you have a hobby you want to describe, a funny story to tell, or a favorite period of history you wish to bring to life, you can use them as inspiration for your animations. But remember to keep the world of your animation consistent. For example, in a silly, comic world, it might make perfect sense for a real hand to enter the frame in and squish your main character, whereas such an action in a realistic setting is likely to break the illusion.

HANDY TIP!

A few cut and shaped strips of colored card stock can be propped up to make layers of hills and mountains or ocean waves. Mount your camera low so you can't see the set's floor in between them. Now you can put a boat, a swimmer, or a giant whale in the gaps between the waves, and they will appear to be in the water.

"WOW" FACTOR!

A CAMERA CAPTURES A 2D IMAGE SO VIEWERS CAN'T TELL WHAT IS CLOSE AND WHAT IS FAR AWAY. TRY LINING UP A NEARBY TOY OR A MODELING CLAY PUPPET WITH A REAL HUMAN WHO IS STANDING FAR AWAY. PRESTO—AN INSTANT SHRINKING EFFECT! USING THIS TECHNIQUE, YOU CAN "HIGH FIVE" AN ACTION FIGURE OR COME FACE TO FACE WITH A TOY RABBIT!

ALWAYS "BUILD TO CAMERA"

As you build your set, always look through your camera's viewfinder to see what your camera sees. Pay close attention to whether the details will be hidden behind other objects or be too small to capture before spending lots of time on them. This is known as "building to camera."

I once spent a whole day making tiny fruits and vegetables for a shop window. In the final film, the audience could only see them as out-of-focus blobs of color. If I'd "built to camera," I would have realized early on that I could have simply scribbled them on a piece of paper for the same effect! Having said that, don't be afraid of adding tiny details if they can be seen—after all, it is the details that make people really believe in the world you have created.

SOUND EFFECTS

Sound is an important part of any animation. Even in the early days of cinema, "silent" films were usually accompanied by soundtracks, performed live by musicians in the theater.

Most animation software features simple sound effects and longer audio clips that you can add to your movie. Check out the software's user guides online and search for "audio features." To add more complicated sounds, take a look at Super Skill 10: Putting It All Together.

SHOOT FROM ABOVE

There is a whole different area of stop-motion we have yet to explore! There is a special technique to make two-dimensional animation using the stop-motion techniques you have learned so far. You position the camera above your stage, and make the action happen in the flat world you create beneath it.

CUTOUT ANIMATION

On pages 6–9 you made a flip book, which is a form of 2D (two-dimensional) animation. Another kind of 2D animation is cutout animation. By laying out cutout paper puppets on a flat surface and filming from above, animators are free from the restrictions of gravity. They can make characters leap, fly, and balance on one leg without the need for a flying rig!

The explosions you created on pages 34–35 are examples of cutout animation. You can use the same technique to animate figures made from colored paper and images cut from magazines. You'll flatten your scene on the table, with the camera looking straight down upon it.

"WOW" FACTOR!

THE "SHOOT FROM ABOVE" TECHNIQUE WAS USED BY TERRY GILLIAM TO MAKE HIS FAMOUS ANIMATIONS FOR *MONTY PYTHON* AND BY RUSSIAN ANIMATION MASTER YURI NORSTEIN TO MAKE HIS CHILDREN'S TALE *HEDGEHOG IN THE FOG*. LOTTE REINIGER USED THE SAME METHOD TO MAKE HER FAMOUS FAIRY TALE SILHOUETTE FILM, *THE ADVENTURES OF PRINCE ACHMED*, IN THE 1920s.

HANDY TIP!

Don't feel limited to flat card stock just because you are shooting from above. See what things are lying around the house that could be used in your setting. A small plastic fork could make an unusual arm, or a pair of buttons might make eyes. Remember to ask first before borrowing objects.

How To Make The Set

When working with cutout animation, you make your set using a method called "collage." Collage involves creating one large image by gluing together several other images and objects in a different order.

WHAT YOU NEED:

- Large sheet of sketching paper as background
- Mixed colors of printer or construction paper
- Scissors
- Paper glue or craft glue
- Box studio (see page 29)
- Cardboard lid for your box studio

MAKE IT BIG

Using a big sheet of sketching paper as your background leaves plenty of space for the action to unfold.

KEEP IT SIMPLE

For your first attempt, make a plain background so that your characters can be clearly seen.

STICK IT DOWN

Stick the background elements down firmly, so you don't knock them out of position while moving characters.

PLAN AHEAD

Plan out the action before you begin. For example, if your story requires an open doorway, make sure to cut it out before you start shooting.

TRY THIS!

How about making your own movie that stars famous Hollywood actors or pokes fun at silly celebrities? Cut out pictures of them from magazines (remember to ask first) to use as figures. You can also add your own speech bubbles to the scene.

REMEMBER TO CHECK THE SIZE OF YOUR CUTOUTS BEFORE ADDING ANY DETAIL BY PUTTING THEM UNDER THE CAMERA TO SEE HOW THEY FIT ON SCREEN.

NOW FOR FIGURES!

Now it's time to make your flat characters move across the flat set. Just as you did with your claymation puppet, you can make a separate body, arms, legs, and head. Once you've created your characters, you'll be ready to animate!

Making Characters

Keep your characters' bodies simple, using basic cutout shapes. The character shown here is about 6 inches tall and made from two different colors of card stock.

Make three different shaped legs: one bent leg, one leg with the foot angled so it's leaning forward, and one leg leaning slightly back.

HANDY TIP!
People often use paper fasteners to attach limbs to bodies, but they don't work very well for animation. Instead, a pinch of mounting putty will stop limbs from moving by accident and makes it possible to swap one shape for another.

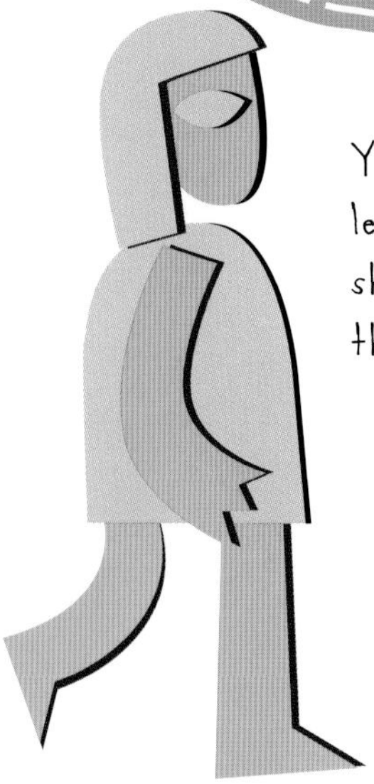

You can adjust the legs in the sequence shown here to make the character walk.

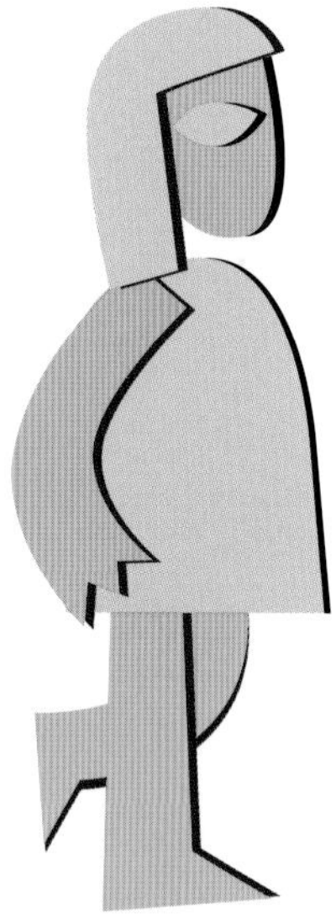

Curved rectangles are best for bent arms and legs.

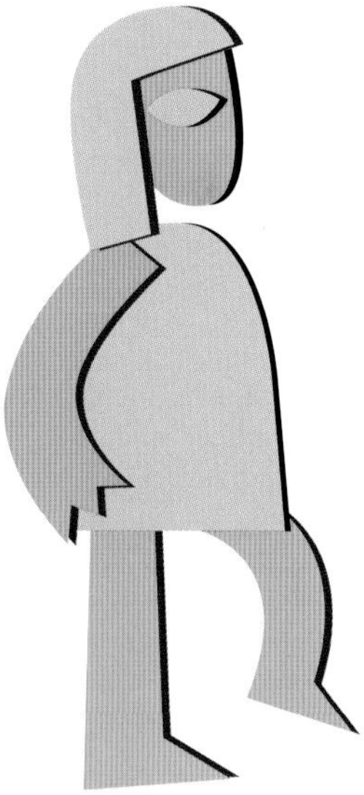

Making Faces

You can bring out your characters' personalities by adding detail to their faces. Make a simple face shape, and cut out several types of eyes, noses, and mouths. Then begin mixing and matching the cutouts to create different expressions.

HANDY TIP!

Make the whites of the eyes and the colored parts (the irises) separately. That way you can make the eyes look up, down, left, and right. It's amazing how much personality eye movement can give your model.

You can also cut out the heads of celebrities or athletes from magazines. If you can find multiple images of the same person's head, try swapping them between frames to give them a variety of expressions.

Rectangles are best for straight arms and legs.

HANDY TIP!

Swapping shapes is the key to making complex moves with ease. It would be challenging to animate a fist opening if you tried to make each finger separately. If you simply swap hand shapes, so frame 1 is a fist and frame 2 is an open hand, it becomes super simple.

TIME FOR THE CAMERA!

So now you have your set and characters, but how do you hold your camera over the flat collage? You build a stand for it, of course! Here's how to make a stand that fits inside your box studio. It's a tricky task even for those with super-duper craft skills, so make this only if you enjoy the challenge of building things. Or ask an adult to help you.

HANDY TIP!

If you haven't made the box studio from Super Skill 5, there are other ways to hold your camera steady over a flat set. You could tape your device to the edge of a table so it looks over it, or use a stool that has a hole in the seat. Improvisation is a big part of animation!

WHAT YOU NEED:

- Corrugated cardboard box
- Ruler or measuring tape
- Pencil
- Large scissors or craft knife
- Strong double-sided tape
- Flexible desk lamp

Step 1

Make the stand by referring to the template in the illustration below. You will need three measurements: the length of the inside of your studio box from front to back, the width of the box, and the height your camera device must be to see most of the bottom of the box.

1 Place your artwork inside the box and hold your camera above it until you can see the entire image. Mark the height.

2 Cut out a large piece of cardboard using the measurements in the image to the right.

3 Lightly score where your folds should be (see image below) with rounded craft scissors or the edge of a plastic ruler for a nice clean fold.

4 Make sure your folded stand fits snuggly in your studio box (see Step 3 on the next page), and make any necessary adjustments.

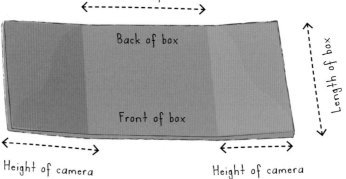

Width of box
Back of box
Length of box
Front of box
Height of camera
Height of camera

Step 2

Next you need to fit your camera device to the stand.

1 Make a hole large enough for your camera lens to see through.

2 Cut a new piece of cardboard the same size as the top of your stand. You might need to ask an adult for help.

3 Trace the outline of your camera device in the center of the new cardboard piece and cut it out, making sure the camera lens lines up with the hole in the stand.

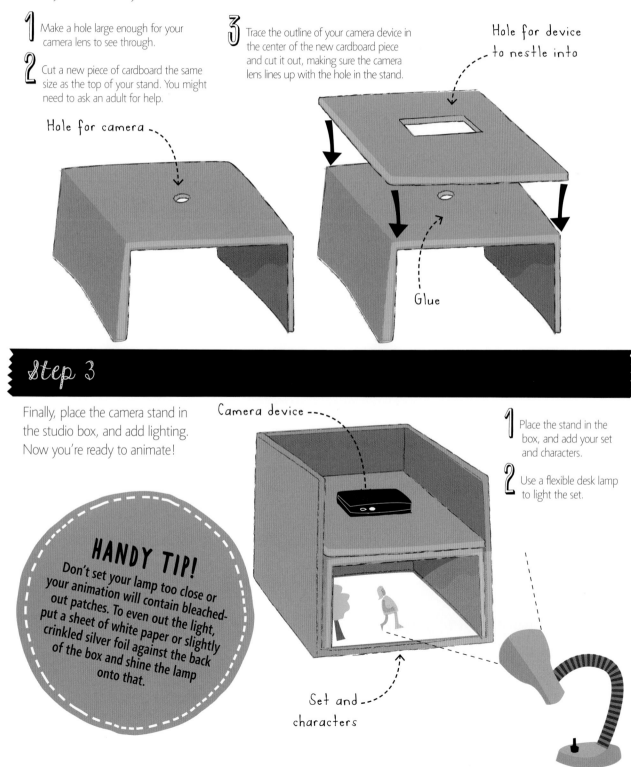

Hole for device to nestle into

Hole for camera

Glue

Step 3

Finally, place the camera stand in the studio box, and add lighting. Now you're ready to animate!

Camera device

1 Place the stand in the box, and add your set and characters.

2 Use a flexible desk lamp to light the set.

HANDY TIP!
Don't set your lamp too close or your animation will contain bleached-out patches. To even out the light, put a sheet of white paper or slightly crinkled silver foil against the back of the box and shine the lamp onto that.

Set and characters

FURTHER ADVENTURES IN 2D

Now it's time to try whiteboard and sand animation, which are both 2D animation techniques. They both involve adding and taking away marks to create movement, but each technique achieves a different look. Whiteboard animation is very sharp and clear, whereas sand animation is soft with a dreamy quality.

WHITEBOARD ANIMATION

Whiteboard animation is among the quickest and least fussy ways to animate. Check out the popular film *Minilogue—Hitchhiker's Choice* online or type "whiteboard animation" into a search engine and you'll see some inspirational examples.

A common mistake in whiteboard animation is completing a movement in too few frames and ending up with animation that jumps from the start to the end of the action, with little movement in between. Be patient as you draw. Focus on creating a flowing motion rather than the finished drawing.

WHAT YOU NEED:

- Whiteboard—anything from letter to poster size (use any white wipe-clean surface that will fit in the bottom of the studio box if you do not have a whiteboard to use)
- Whiteboard marker
- Tissue or wet wipes

HANDY TIP!
Work slowly and methodically. It's easy to focus too much on the drawing and then forget to click the capture button!

Try it out

Let's start with a quick experiment to learn how the whiteboard animation technique works. After the experiment, you should end up with a mark that travels across the screen and branches out before splitting into two marks. Once you feel comfortable, you can try out some ideas of your own.

◦ Make a mark on the whiteboard, just an inch or so long, and capture the frame.

◦ Wipe away the tail end of the mark with a wet wipe, tissue, or your finger (see frame 1). Add to the line, making the changes small until you're used to the speed of it (see frame 2).

◦ Use the onion skinning feature to keep track of how much the image changes from frame to frame.

◦ Keep adding to the front end of the mark and taking away from the tail (see frame 3). Grow the mark by adding more than you take away, and shrink it again by taking away more than you add.

"WOW" FACTOR!

USE DIFFERENT COLORED PENS TO CREATE A RANGE OF EFFECTS. TRY TO INTRODUCE MEANING TO THE DIFFERENT COLORS. FOR EXAMPLE, YOU COULD TURN YOUR ANIMATION INTO A DANCE OR A FIGHT BETWEEN THE COLORS BLUE AND RED.

◦ As you move the mark forward, create variety by growing it and shrinking it. But don't switch too abruptly or you'll risk creating jerky movements.

◦ Add a branch to the mark, so when you wipe away the end, the mark splits into two (see frame 4).

◦ See how many branches you can draw before you lose control of the marks and their movements.

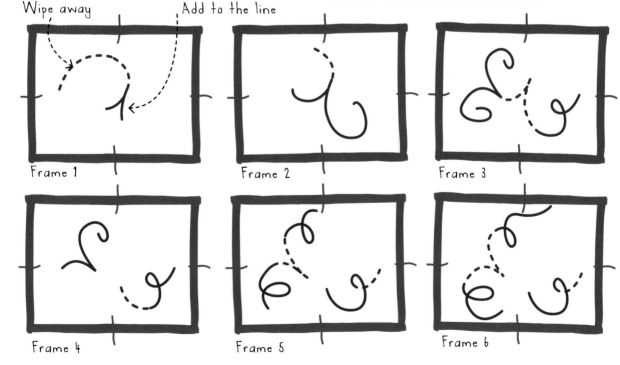

Wipe away   Add to the line

Frame 1   Frame 2   Frame 3

Frame 4   Frame 5   Frame 6

SAND ANIMATION

"Sand animation" is a soft and flowing form of animation. It is great for telling dreamy stories and making natural forms. This technique is used to great effect by the Canadian animator Caroline Leaf in a film called *The Owl Who Married a Goose*. It is a very sad story but definitely worth a watch. You can find a link for it on page 62.

SHINING LIGHT THROUGH SAND

For this animation technique, you need a clear plastic box or tray to hold the sand, a light to shine beneath it, and a way to hold your camera device steady above it. The sand in the bottom of the box blocks out the light. But when you make a mark in the sand, the light shines through, making the marked part appear lighter against the dark background.

You can make a cardboard stand just like the one you made for your cutout animation. If you'd rather not make another stand, you can support your sand-filled box between two tables and shine the lamp underneath it. Use a tripod to support your camera device above the sand.

WHAT YOU NEED:

- Corrugated cardboard box
- Large clear plastic box or tray
- Large scissors
- Dry sand or flour
- Flexible desk lamp

THE SAND ANIMATION SETUP

Make a sandbox stand like the camera device stand featured on pages 50 and 51. The sandbox stand will sit underneath your camera device stand in the box studio, supporting a transparent box underneath your camera.

Camera device

Transparent box

Sand

HANDY TIP!
Flour gives a similar effect as sand but is slightly harder to control.

BE CAREFUL!
DO NOT LOOK DIRECTLY AT YOUR DESK LAMP, EVEN THROUGH THE SAND. ALWAYS SET THE LAMP TO ONE SIDE.

Try Different Tools

You can make marks in the sand with your fingers or cotton swabs. If you are not using much sand, try sweeping it with a brush to form interesting shapes and unique effects.

Experiment With Sand

Start without sand in the tray. Let sand flow from your palm, a little at a time, to create shapes that grow and spread from frame to frame.

Use Stencils

You can create simple characters with sand by using stencils. Cut your character's shape out of a piece of card stock that is just a little bigger than the character itself. Put the card stock on your surface, and pour sand into the cutout. Carefully lift the card stock to leave the character's shape formed in sand.

No sand   Sand

Areas thickly covered in sand will be dark, while space with little or no sand will be light.

WELL DONE!

You've nearly reached the end of the animation Super Skills. There is one more chapter about editing, but you have now learned all the classic animation skills and know how to avoid common mistakes.

PUTTING IT ALL TOGETHER

You don't have to edit shots together to make a movie. You can plan out your movie and shoot each scene separately, or tell the whole story from a single camera position. But editing can make your movie so much better and help you take out the mistakes. For example, you can cut away from a great shot of a killer robot just before your brother put his hand into the shot and knocked it over. You can also use editing to switch scenes and add dramatic music—editing allows you to get really creative!

BUILDING IT UP

Once you have taken enough frames to produce some continuous movement, you've made a "shot." Put together a few shots, and you have a "scene." Put the scenes together and start editing your own short movie!

CHOOSING EDITING SOFTWARE

To edit your shots, you need some basic editing software. This will allow you to work with whole shots and scenes, as well as add effects such as music. Windows, Linux, and Apple computer operating systems have free software installed for editing home movies, and that's all you need. Look at the chart below to check which software to look for on your computer.

HANDY TIP!
Editing can be scary. Don't be afraid to ask an adult to help you. You'll definitely want to look at online tutorials available for the particular software you'll be using.

OPERATING SYSTEM		EDITING SOFTWARE
• Apple	⟶	iMovie
• Windows	⟶	Windows Movie Maker
• Linux	⟶	Movie Gimp

EXPORTING YOUR CLIPS

Before you edit your shots or clips, you need to convert the clips in your animation software into a movie or file format that your editing software will understand. Your app should have a "Share" or "Export" button for creating a version of the movie that works outside the app. You have the option to publish straight to a site such as YouTube, but if you want to put more than one movie file together, you'll need to Export or Share them to your device's "Camera Roll," "Video Library," or "iTunes."

Once you have exported your shots or clips to one of those locations, you can plug your device into your computer and upload them to your hard drive. It's a good idea to create one folder where you keep all the files that make up your film.

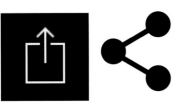

The icons above are typically used for "Export" and "Share."

Your animation app's Export or Share screen will look something like this. The icons that lead directly to each website.

HANDY TIP!

Animation professionals are very careful about keeping files organized. They often have a project folder for each movie, a separate folder inside that for each scene, and another folder for audio. They also give each movie file a clearly identifiable shot number or name.

DIGITAL FILES

Each animation project you have shot will become a "movie file," "movie clip," or "video file" when you export it. Those are all names for the same thing—a digital file containing moving images. Most apps will only export a movie file format called "Mp4," which works in most editing software.

FEATURES OF EDITING SOFTWARE

You will find that different editing programs have their own way of showing the same features. If only things were simple. But fear not! They all work on the same principle and contain the same basic elements.

THE PROJECT WINDOW

One of the main areas of your software contains the files that make up the movie—your shots. Sometimes this window is labeled "Media," sometimes it's called the "Project window," "Assets," "Events," or "Clip bin." You can import movie files into this window by dragging the files onto it from where they are stored on your computer. If this doesn't work, use the "File > Import" menu.

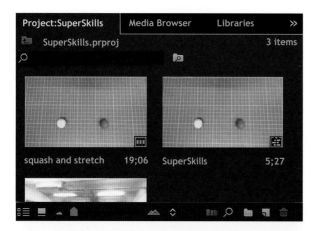

THE TIMELINE

You also have a "Timeline," which is the area where you put the shots together, one after the other like words in a sentence. You drag your files into the timeline. You will be familiar with a timeline from your stop-motion software. But don't forget, in the editing software timeline, you are dealing with movie clips, not individual frames.

Sometimes the editing timeline is an empty line that runs along the bottom of the screen. Other times it is more like the lines in a book, running from left to right with one on top of the other, becoming longer as you add to it.

THE VIEWING WINDOW

As you add shots to your timeline, you will be able to watch your work in progress in a "Viewing window." This is often the largest panel on the screen.

The images on this page are of a "Project window" panel and the "Timeline" panel from a software program called *Adobe Premiere*.

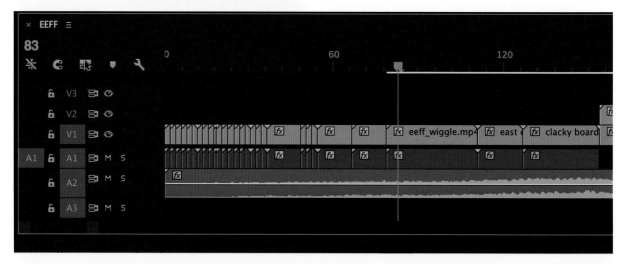

Project window

Menu bar

Viewing window

Timeline

Audio

The image above is a typical editing software screen.

AUDIO

"Audio," or sound, usually sits in a separate line in the timeline, underneath the video. Most editing software will come with a large library of sound effects and free-to-use music loops. You can add to these by recording your own sound effects or by visiting online sound libraries (see page 62 for some links).

ATMOS

There is a useful idea in sound design called "Atmosphere," or "Atmos" for short. It refers to the general sounds we're usually unaware of that make up the character of any space, like the hum of distant traffic, birds singing, or people muttering.

It's a good term to know when you're searching through a sound effects library. Try starting with this sort of background sound, dragging it into position under part of your animation. You can then add shorter sound effects, such as the crashes and bangs of the action, on top of the atmosphere sounds. This layering of sounds will make your animation sound more real.

THERE IS NEVER REALLY SILENCE, ANYWHERE IN THE WORLD. EVEN IN THE QUIETEST PLACE YOU WILL BE ABLE TO HEAR THE SOUNDS OF YOUR BREATHING AND YOUR HEARTBEAT!

EDITING YOUR ANIMATIONS

Every software has its own way of doing things, so in these pages we've provided a general guide. The most useful advice when it comes to editing is to be organized, take your time, and back up your original files.

Step 1: BRINGING YOUR SHOTS TOGETHER

Once your files are organized into one project folder on your computer, change the names and number them so it's easy to determine which order they should appear.

Some software copies a movie into the project, so it is stored inside the project, whatever happens to the original file. Other software relies on the movie being where it was before you dragged it in and having the same name. In either case, it's good to put everything into one folder and save the project there too.

Step 2: OPEN YOUR EDITING SOFTWARE

Drag your files to the project window, or go to File > Import Movie. Now you can drag the files into the timeline, placing them in the correct order.

If you have a storyboard, you can tick off shots as you add them to the timeline. You have now created the "rough cut" edit of your masterpiece! Great job! Watch the play back, and take a break.

Step 3: EDITING CLIPS

You can adjust the speed of your clip, usually by right clicking on it and going to "Speed/Duration" or by using a slider. Changing the speed to 200% will make it run twice as fast, changing it to 50% will make it run at half speed.

If you hover over the end of a clip, you can drag the end, or "out point," shorter to cut off the end of the clip.

This is useful if something spoiled the end of the shot or if you shot more than you need.

If you need to cut in the middle of your clip, use the razor blade tool. You might want to do this if there is a stray hand in the shot or to insert a different shot into the scene.

TRANSITIONS

There will be lots of interesting transitions to choose from. A transition is the change from one scene to another. So you can have one clip wiping across the screen or becoming a star shape to reveal the next scene. Use transitions to represent things you cannot animate easily, such as showing time has passed or that you are traveling far away.

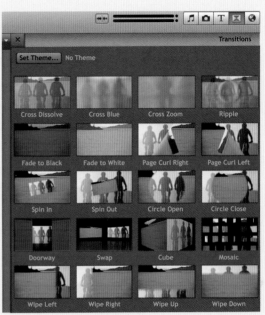

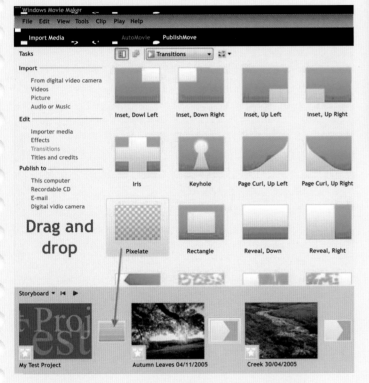

HANDY TIP!
Use transitions sparingly because too many can interrupt the flow of your story.

Step 4: TITLES & CREDITS!

To name your film, click on "Titles" or "Text," and change the text from "Title" to the name of your film. Drag it to the start of the film. Do the same at the end of the film but fill in "Directed and Animated by" with your name! Don't forget to credit anyone who helped you.

NOW THAT YOU'VE PRACTICED ALL THE SKILLS, YOU ARE OFFICIALLY AN ANIMATOR AND WORTHY OF WEARING A SHIRT WITH THE MOTTO "THE MAGIC LIVES BETWEEN THE FRAMES." KEEP ENJOYING THE PROCESS. SEE YOU LATER, ANIMATOR!

USEFUL LINKS

There are lots of great resources online for animators, and hundreds of animations made by first-time animators are uploaded every day. Here are some great animations you can watch online to discover more about the animation process, as well as a selection of useful online resources.

ANIMATIONS

"The Owl Who Married a Goose"
www.nfb.ca/film/owl_who_married_goose
This short animation by Caroline Leaf is based on an Inuit legend. Watch it to learn more about the effects that are possible using sand animation techniques.

"Minilogue—Hitchhiker's Choice"
vimeo.com/158803
This short film is a great example of what you can create using whiteboard animation.

"Her Morning Elegance"
vimeo.com/13781225
This music video by Oren Lavie has been made using stop-motion photography. By using small movements and taking many frames, the animators have created the impression that the actress is walking and swimming.

Rex the Dog: "Bubblicious"
www.youtube.com/watch?v=acay3S2PhSg
This music video was made using stop motion and replacement animation. It's really fun to watch and shows you how the 3D characters were made during the film.

USEFUL RESOURCES

www.stopmotionanimation.com
As you get more advanced in stop-motion animation, you might find it useful to visit this website. There is a huge amount of information and advice from stop-motion supergeeks. It can be overwhelming, but there is also a "Handbook" section that gives newbies a great place to start.

www.sounddogs.com
Sounddogs is a commercial online library of sound effects. Explore the site to see what sounds are available.

www.aardman.com
Aardman is a fantastic stop-motion studio based in Bristol in the UK. They make series and features such as *Wallace & Grommit*, *Morph*, and *Shaun the Sheep* and are famous throughout the world for their claymation work. Their website has clips and info galore.

brickfilms.com
A great way to start making toy animations is with LEGO bricks and other construction toys. Brickfilms is the oldest website hosting films and sharing advice between users. Take a look at the films its members have made. If they inspire you to make your own, you could submit it to the site!

Website information is correct at time of going to press. The publishers cannot accept liability for any information or links found on third-party websites.

GLOSSARY

2D two-dimensional; flat

3D three-dimensional; lumpy! Model animators are sometimes called lumpies by computer animators, a badge that model animators wear with honor

ATMOS atmosphere. The general sounds heard in a space

AUDIO sound

CLAYMATION animation created frame by frame using changes made to modeling clay

CLIP short piece of animation

COLLAGE image made by cutting out other images and gluing them, and sometimes other objects, together in a different order

EDITING assembling and making changes to something

FILE FORMAT a particular way a computer has encoded information

FLYING RIG support structure that allows a puppet to fly

FRAME single still image that is, or will be, part of an animated sequence

FRAME RATE speed in frames per second (fps) that the images in an animation will be played back in

MOVIE moving image

MOVIE FORMAT a particular way a computer has encoded the visual information contained in your animation

ONION SKINNING semi-transparent, ghostly image of the last frame you shot, overlaid onto whatever is in front of the camera now

PIXEL tiny square of color that is used, in their millions, by digital displays to show images

PIXILATION animating the human form; from the same root word as pixie, meaning magic

REPLACEMENT ANIMATION swapping one object with a very similar object to fool the eye into thinking it's the same object that has changed shape

RESOLUTION either the end of a story or the size of a digital image, usually measured in pixels

SCENE everything in a film that happens during one situation, before the set or scenery changes

SHOT everything in a film that happens between the start and end of a sequence of images that are similar enough to give the illusion of one movement

STOP-MOTION animation created by the moving of inanimate objects

TIMELINE visual way of showing how clips or images are spread out over time by laying them out in a line

TRANSITION pre-programmed video effect that changes how one clip changes or cuts to the next

VIDEO digital moving image

INDEX